Steppingstones to Go

Steppingstones
to
Go

by Shigemi Kishikawa

Rutland, Vermont
Charles E. Tuttle Company
Tokyo, Japan

Representatives

For Continental Europe:
BOXERBOOKS, INC., *Zurich*

For the British Isles:
PRENTICE-HALL INTERNATIONAL, INC., *London*

For Australasia:
BOOK WISE (AUSTRALIA) PTY. LTD.
104-108 Sussex Street, Sydney 2000

Published by the Charles E. Tuttle Company, Inc.
of Rutland, Vermont & Tokyo, Japan
with editorial offices at
Suido 1-chome, 2-6, Bunkyo-ku, Tokyo

© 1965 by Charles E. Tuttle Co., Inc.

Library of Congress Catalog Card No. 65-13411

International Standard Book No. 0-8048-0547-4

First printing, 1965
Twelfth printing, 1987

Book design by Simon Virgo
Printed in Japan

Contents

Foreword

Go is a game played by two contestants. The game is played with black and white "stones" on a checkered board. The players are usually classed as strong and weak, based upon degree of knowledge and skill. The stronger player takes the white stones and the weaker player takes the black stones. Handicaps are given the weaker players by mutual agreement before commencement of the game. The game of *go* may be one of the most difficult to learn, but this fact makes the game highly interesting. Once techniques are mastered, the beginner will find it difficult to put the game aside.

Now, let's learn how to play *go* in the following chapters.

·1·

Equipment

The board or *go ban*

The board, or *go ban* as it is called in Japanese, is a solid block of wood, generally about four or five inches thick, resting upon four detachable legs. It is about $17\frac{1}{2}$ inches long and 16 inches wide. The board and legs are usually stained yellow.

The best boards are made of *kaya* (*Torreya Nucifera,* or the famous Torrey pine of California). However, these boards are extremely expensive. Boards are also made of *katsura* (Japanese Judas tree), *icho* (gingko), or *hinoki* (Japanese cypress). *Katsura* boards, reasonable in price, are the most widely used today. Recently, flat boards without legs have been introduced, and are popular because they are more convenient and suitable when the game is played on a table or in a similar position.

The board is crisscrossed by 19 vertical and 19 horizontal lines, forming 361 points of intersection, and there are nine dotted points on its surface. These are called *hoshi* which means star, and they are used by the weaker player in the event of a handicap game. As will be seen,

9

Diagram 1

The surface of *go ban*
showing the nine dotted points called *hoshi*

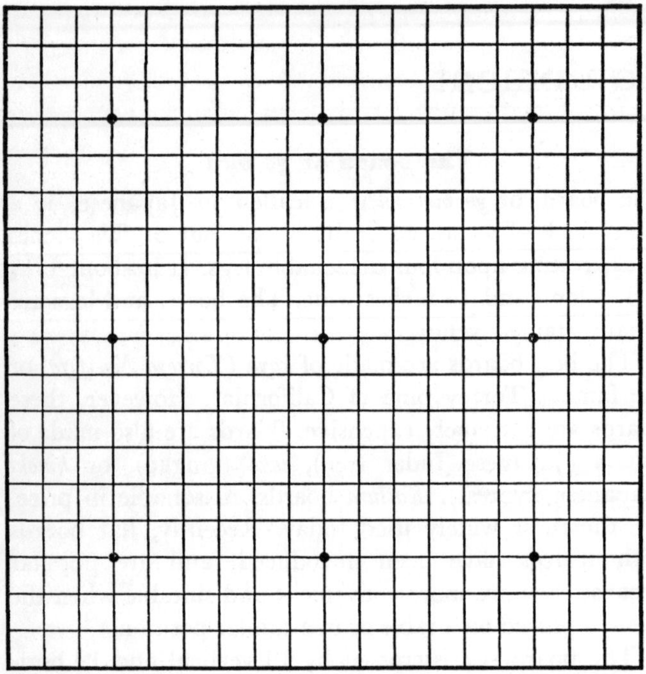

this gives the weaker player an advantage. Diagram 1 shows the surface of a *go ban*.

The stones or *go ishi*

As mentioned above, there are two kinds of stones: white and black. The white stones are made from clamshells that come from Miyazaki Prefecture in Kyushu, the southern part of Japan. They have a lustrous polish and are pleasant to the touch. The black stones are made of a special kind of stone from the Nachi cataract in Kishiu, in central Japan, and are called Nachi *ishi*. As a good set of stones is quite expensive, cheaper stones, made of hard glass, are widely utilized. There are 361 stones, corresponding to the number of the points of intersection on the board. One hundred and eighty are white and the remaining 181 are black. As the weaker player takes the black stones and is entitled to the first move, the extra stone is black. In actual play, about 150 stones of each color are sufficient to play a game. The stones are contained in lacquered boxes or *go ke*.

The stones in play are placed on the points of intersection of the lines and *not* on the squares as in chess. Once placed, they cannot be removed, remaining on the points where they are placed until the end of a game, except when they are captured.

A hint should be given the beginner not to grasp a large handful of stones in one hand and use it to feed the other. Each stone should be withdrawn from the box at the conclusion of the opponent's turn to play and only when it is required for immediate use.

It is not absolutely necessary to learn the correct way to handle stones, but, for your reference, it is as follows:

grasp the stone lightly between middle and index fingers of the right hand, resting it lightly on the nail of the index finger—an act that requires some practice to perform gracefully.

·2·

The Game

The object of the game

The object of *go* is to secure territory as represented by
the number of the unoccupied points of intersection. At
the end of the game, the amount of vacant space is cal-
culated, and the stones that have been captured are used
to fill up the vacant spaces claimed by the opponent.
The winner is the player who has succeeded in occupying
the larger territory after the captured stones are used in
this way.

With this ultimate object in view, two plans of action
are followed, one being simply to rail off space by forming
walls of stones around the area which the player desires
to occupy, and the other that of capturing the stones or
space of the opponent. However, if the players merely
fence in parts of the board regardless of each other's play,
a dull and monotonous game results. More interesting
games develop when the players, in their efforts to secure
territory, attack each other's stones or space, as will be
explained later. The game is concluded when neither
player is able to secure further unoccupied territory and

when neither is willing to hazard further attacks on the territory already surrounded by his opponent.

The rules of play

Black plays first, placing one of his stones on any intersection on the board. Thereafter Black and White play alternately.

Aside from some rules relating to specific situations (explained later), all the necessary basic rules to play *go* are as follows:

1. The board must be so placed that the narrow sides are immediately opposite each player.

2. The stones are played on the points of intersection of the lines. As mentioned in Chapter 1, once placed they are not moved except when captured or for counting purposes at the end of the game.

3. With evenly matched players, the right of first move is decided by having one player hold a handful of stones and his opponent calling odd or even. If the opponent guesses correctly, he wins the black stones, and has the advantage of playing first.

4. When players are not evenly matched, the weaker player is given a handicap and he uses the black stones. In this case, White has the first move, and Rule 3 is ignored.

5. When all of the intersections adjacent to a stone or a group of stones are occupied by stones of the opponent, that stone or group of stones is captured and removed from the board.

6. It is forbidden to play on any point which is completely surrounded by the opponent's stones and there is only the one point vacant, unless the play results in the

capture of all or part of the surrounding stones, because no stone may remain on the board if it is completely surrounded by stones of the opposite color.

7. If a group of stones contains two separate "eyes" (explained in detail in Chapter 6), it is permanently safe from capture, regardless of the enemy stones surrounding the group.

8. In a *ko* position (described in detail in Chapter 9), a player cannot repeat his previous move without first playing at some other part of the board.

9. To arrive at the final score, White counts the points within Black's territory and Black counts White's. To facilitate counting, the respective territories should be arranged as far as possible in rows of tens and twenties. Stones may be transferred from one place to any other place for this purpose.

Observers are not supposed to make comments. Even nowadays boards with four legs have a hollow on the reverse side in which in olden times the gory head of the interfering bystander was placed as a hint to others.

It is usually considered impolite to make the first move upon the central point of the board except in handicap games. At the end of the game, the stones should be returned to each player and not left in position.

Although not a part of the rules of the game, it seems appropriate here to describe briefly the purpose of handicaps. Before commencing play, handicaps are given by the stronger player in order to equalize the game between the two contestants. The placing of handicaps is shown in Diagrams 2–9.

Though only nine points are marked on the board, handicaps of 13, 17, and even 21 are given by advanced players to beginners. However, handicaps larger than nine stones are seldom practicable. Therefore, the nine-stone handicap is ordinarily the recognized maximum.

In the beginning, progress at playing *go* is very rapid, and handicaps are reduced very quickly. Usually, four, or sometimes three, wins cause a decrease of one stone in the handicap allowed. When handicaps are given, Black loses his right to first move since he has the advantage of stones already on the board.

Diagram 2

A two-stone handicap

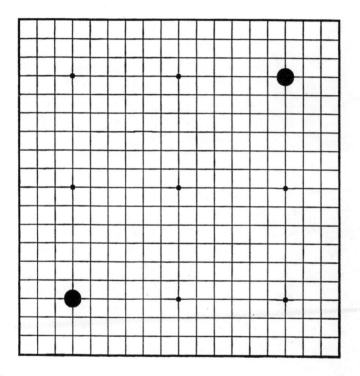

Diagram 3

A three-stone handicap

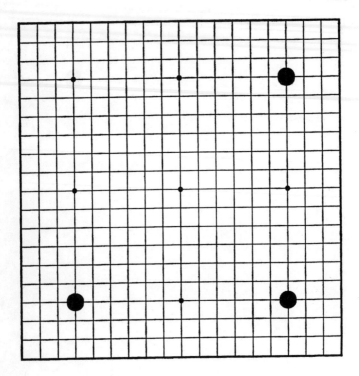

Diagram 4

A four-stone handicap

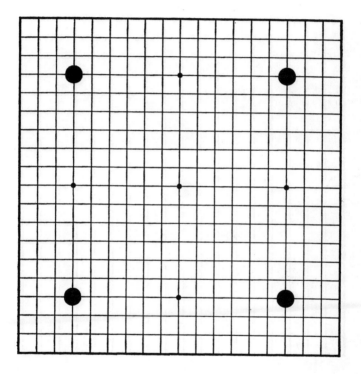

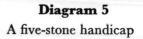

Diagram 5

A five-stone handicap

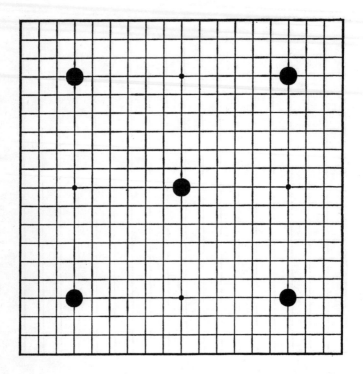

Diagram 6

A six-stone handicap

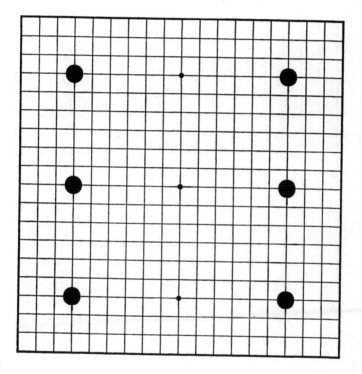

Diagram 7

A seven-stone handicap

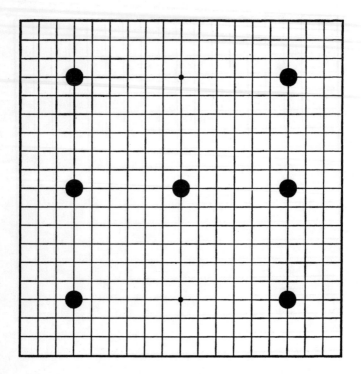

Diagram 8

An eight-stone handicap

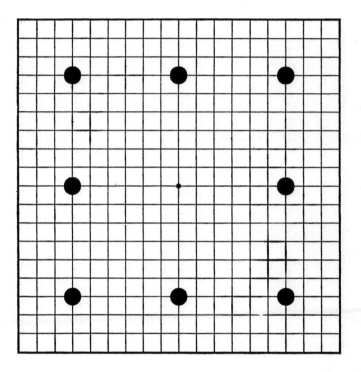

Diagram 9

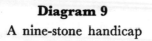

A nine-stone handicap

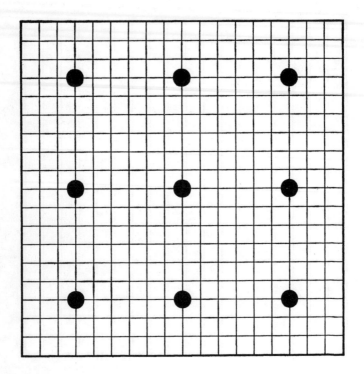

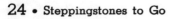

•3•

Territory

In the preceding chapter you learned that the primary object of *go* is to secure territory with your stones. The vacant areas surrounded by the players' stones are called territories, and each point of intersection is counted as one point in the possessor's favor. Let's study the diagram shown overleaf.

Each of the vacant areas surrounded by the four groups of stones in Diagram 10 is territory belonging to Black and White respectively. The two White groups have 25 points of territory and the two Black groups have 19 points of territory. Thus, it is apparent that the territory is the area which is completely surrounded by connected stones of the same color. In actual games, a number of independent territories like these is usually formed by each contestant. Diagram 11 shows another typical form of territory, although it is far from any actual game. It may seem to you that White's territory in the center of the board is larger than that of Black who controls the outside area of the board, but it is not because Black has 140 points of intersection (the entire outer border), and

Diagram 10

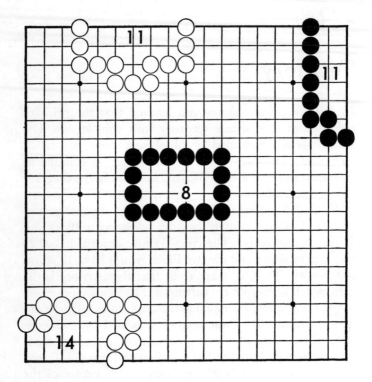

White has only 121 points of intersection. The diagram indicates that acquiring territory on the corners is most important since it can be secured more easily than any other place and with less stones. This will be explained in more detail in Chapter 11.

Diagram 11

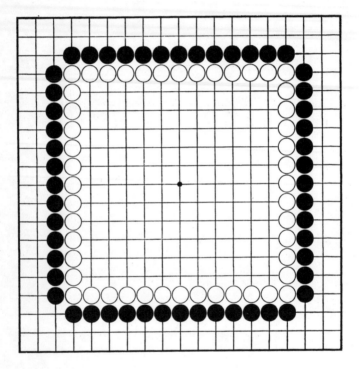

• 4 •

Connection and Disconnection

The black and white stones are often likened to two opposing armies on a battlefield. When they are separated or cut off from their own lines they are more easily attacked and captured by the enemy.

Two or more stones of the same color can be connected into a single unit by placing them on intersections of vertical and horizontal lines. Connection is made diagonally only under certain conditions, as will be learned later. Look at Diagram 12, Figures A and B. All of the black stones are securely connected with each other. However, in the case of Figure C, the black stones are not connected. They have been cut off by White, and are in a disconnected position. Of course, the white stones in this situation are disconnected as well as the black.

Diagrams 13 and 14 illustrate how connection and disconnection may actually occur. In Diagram 13, if Black plays 1 as shown in Figure B, all the black stones will be connected. However, if it is White's turn to play and he plays 1 as indicated in Figure C, all the black stones will be disconnected into two separate groups.

Diagram 12

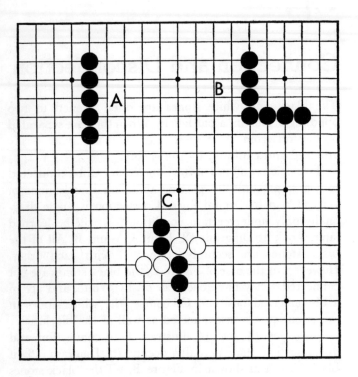

Diagram 13

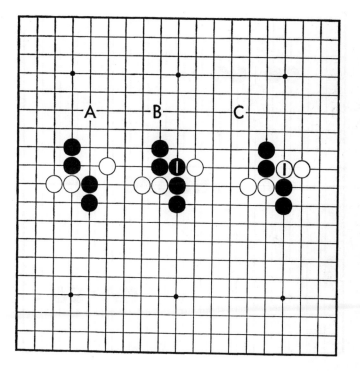

Diagram 14

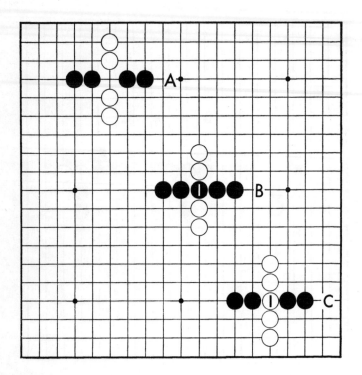

Diagram 15

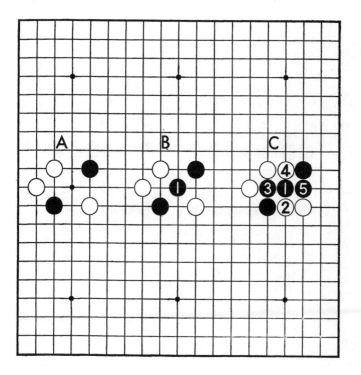

Diagram 16

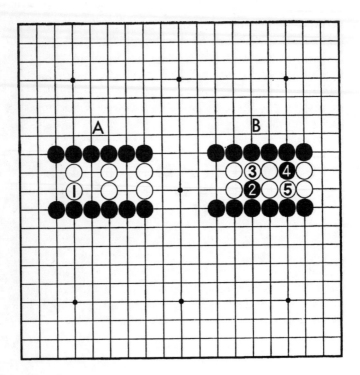

In Diagram 14, where is the Black supposed to play in order to connect his own stones into a single unit?

There is no place to play other than 1 as indicated in Figure B. If White is to play first, on the contrary, he plays 1 just as Black did in Figure B and thus succeeds in disconnecting the black stones as indicated in Figure C.

Stones aligned diagonally are also considered as connected under certain conditions. Diagram 15 is an example of this situation. If Black is to play first, he plays 1 as indicated in Figure B and thus can connect his two stones. In this situation, there is no way for White to disconnect the black stones because the sequence thereof will be as shown in Figure C.

Another example of stones not actually connected but which cannot be prevented from connecting can be seen in Diagram 16. In Figure B, White has connected diagonally by playing 3 and 5.

In the examples, play has been indicated on certain points of intersection. However, a little study will reveal that the same final situation will prevail regardless of which of the pertinent points of intersection is chosen for the first play.

In other words, any form of stones can be considered as connected if there is no way for either Black or White to effect disconnection by an alternate play.

Diagram 17

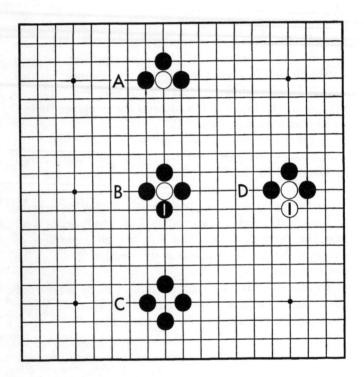

·5·

Capture

As briefly explained in Chapter 2, the player who so completely surrounds his opponent that no vacant point is left in the enclosure gains all the stones thus surrounded. Each stone captured is regarded as a penalty point to the value of one against the loser. When a player sees that capture of his stones is almost inevitable, he usually abandons for the moment the attempt to save them and plays at some more profitable point. Often by this method he is able to effect their rescue and even capture the attacking stones. Captured stones are called *hama*.

Diagram 17 shows the fundamental form of capture. As it stands in Figure A, the lone white stone is found in a position which will be completely surrounded by Black's next move. A stone or group of stones in this position is said to be in check. If it is Black's turn to play in this situation, he plays 1 as shown in Figure B and can capture and remove the one white stone from the board. Figure C shows the final position after the white stone was captured and removed from the board.

On the contrary, however, if White is to play first in

Diagram 18

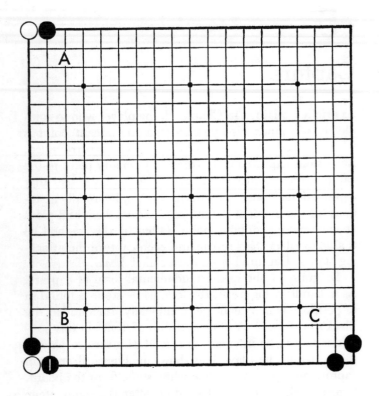

Diagram 19

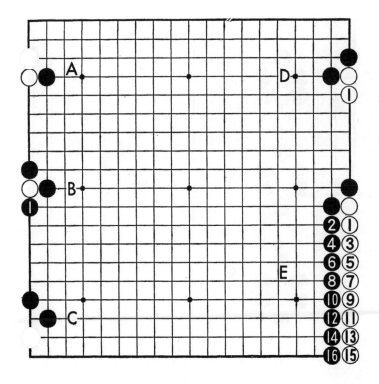

Diagram 20

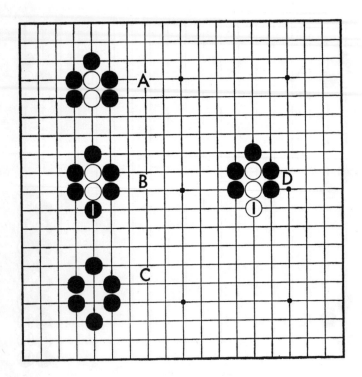

the initial position, he plays 1 as indicated in Figure D and thereby escapes immediate capture.

A stone placed on the edge of the board is different in situation since the outer lines act as a boundary completing the enclosure. In the case of Diagram 18, if it is Black's turn to play, he plays 1 as shown in Figure B and thereby completes the enclosure, resulting in capture and removal of the white stone from the board. Figure C shows the position after the removal has taken place.

Diagram 19 is similar in form to the one shown in Diagram 18. The lone white stone on the edge of the board in Figure A is in check as it stands. If it is Black's turn to play, he plays 1 as shown in Figure B and thereby can capture the one white stone (Figure C). Even if White is to play first as in Figure D, the result will be the same. White may extend along the line, but each move on the part of White will be followed by a corresponding pursuing move by Black as indicated in Figure E, capturing all the white stones upon reaching the corner of the board.

In Diagram 20, Figure A, two white stones are in check. If Black plays 1 as shown in Figure B, he can capture the two white stones and remove them from the board. Figure C indicates the final position after removal. If, on the other hand, White is to play first, he must obviously extend at 1 as shown in Figure D, thereby escaping.

In Diagram 21, Figure A shows a greater number of stones in check and how they are captured. The manner of play is exactly the same as the others previously explained. If Black plays 1 as shown in Figure B, he can capture the three white stones. Figure C is the final position. If, however, White has the first play, he can save the stones from capture by extending at 1 as in Figure D.

Diagram 21

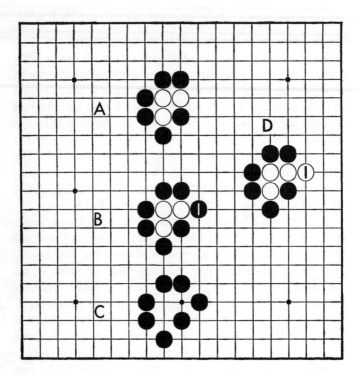

Diagram 22

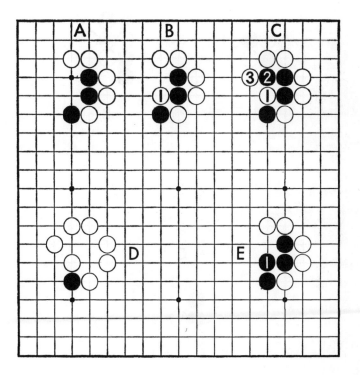

Diagram 23

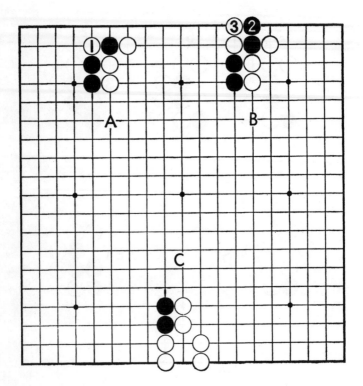

Diagram 24

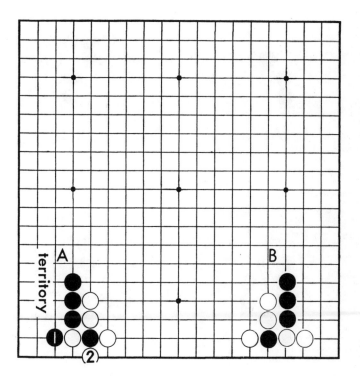

Diagram 25

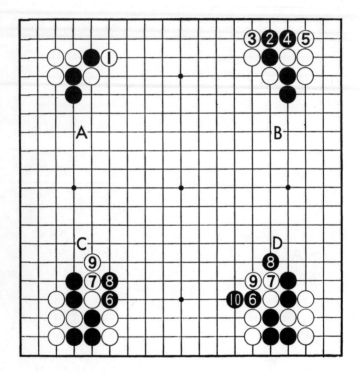

The two black stones in Diagram 22, Figure A, are partly surrounded by White. If White plays first, Black cannot save his two stones from capture. Figures B and C show the capturing process and the final position after removal is shown in Figure D. On the contrary, however, if Black plays first he can save his two stones by connecting them to his outer stone as indicated in Figure E.

In Diagram 23, Figure A, if one black stone is cut off by White as shown therein, there is no way to defend it. Even if Black tries to escape by extending at 2 as in Figure B, capture is obvious, and the two black stones are removed from the board as in Figure C. Therefore, if it is Black's turn to play, he plays 1 as shown in Diagram 24, Figure A and lets White take the one black stone, thereby acquiring his territory on the left side. If Black fails to do so, White usually extends his stones towards the corner as shown in Figure B without taking one black stone (it can be captured any time) and advances into Black's territory. Consequently, it must always be remembered that losses must be minimized.

Look at Diagrams 25 and 26. These are much more complicated situations concerning capture. If White plays correctly as indicated in the process of Diagram 25, he will be able to capture the black stones without fail, but if he plays as shown in Diagram 26, Black finds his way of escape and cannot be captured, resulting in figures as indicated. From these examples, study the direction in which to place your stones so as to prevent the opponent's escape. These tactics will be set forth in detail later.

Diagram 26

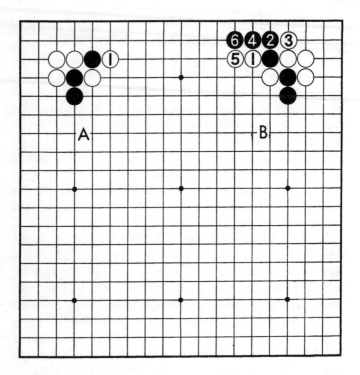

A   B

· 6 ·

Life and Death

If a group of stones contains two or more separate
"eyes" it is safe and cannot be captured, though it is
completely surrounded by the opponent. The reason is
that to play on any point which is completely surrounded
by the opponent's stones is prohibited unless the play
results in the capture of all or part of the surrounding
stones. This is a result of the rule for surrounding and
taking stones and not a separate rule. It follows necessarily
from the method by which stones are captured. It is the
most important principle of the game.

In order to understand the rule of the "eye," you must
first examine the situation shown in Diagram 27, Figure
A. The vacant point in the center of the white group is
the eye which is called *me* in Japanese. However, any
group of stones must have at least two eyes to be secure,
and one eye alone is useless. For instance, if the white
group in this diagram is completely surrounded by Black
as shown in Figure B, the whole white group is killed by
Black by playing at 1. Figure C shows the final position
after the white group is removed from the board.

Diagram 27

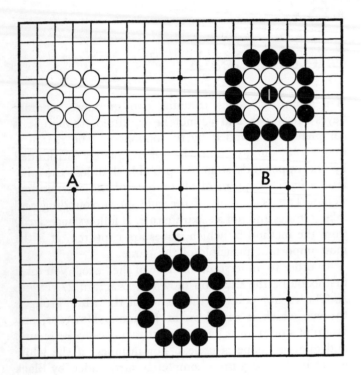

Diagram 28

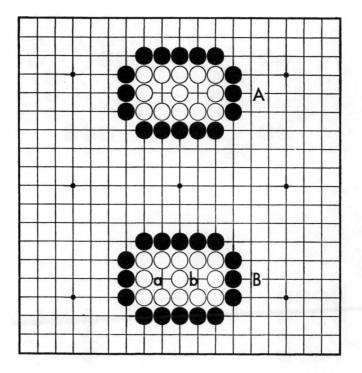

Diagram 29

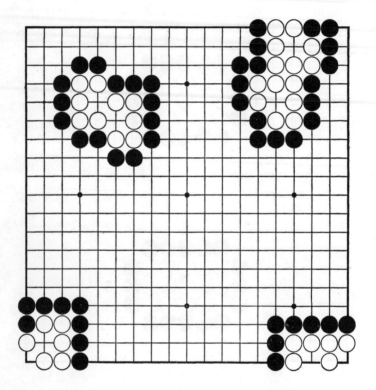

Diagram 28 shows a safe group containing two separate eyes. The white group shown in Figure A is perfectly secure although it has been completely surrounded by the Black. The reason why the group is permanently safe is because even if a black stone could be played on *one* of the vacant intersections—"a" *or* "b"—there still remains one space yet to be filled in order to effect capture. The rule against playing on a point surrounded by the opponent's stones *unless capture can thereby be effected* is applicable and prevents this play. The black stone itself would be dead as soon as it touched the board, and hence it would be impossible to surround this group of white stones unless two stones were played at once. The white stones, therefore, cannot be surrounded or captured. This is the principle of the two eyes. In other words, a safe group is defined as the group of stones containing two vacant points on which play is forbidden.

Diagram 29 shows some other examples of safe groups of stones. Each of them contains two separate eyes and is perfectly secure at all times. It makes no difference whether the vacant eyes are situated on the edges or in the corners of the board or how far from each other they may be.

Beginners frequently form groups containing false eyes which are called *kageme*. *Kage* means "chipped" or "incomplete." By a false eye is meant a vacant point which must be occupied in order to prevent capture by the opponent's completion of a cordon at that point.

Examine Diagram 30, Figure A. At a glance, this white group seems to have two eyes, but if you look at it carefully you can see that three white stones are in check since they are not connected to the remainder. If a black stone is

Diagram 30

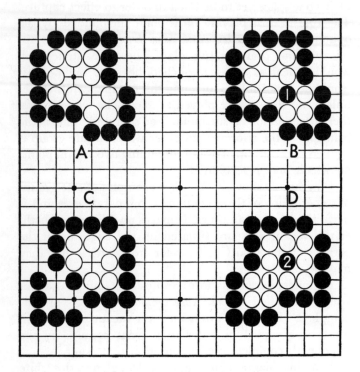

played at 1 as shown in Figure B, it can capture three stones and remove them from the board, resulting in the situation shown in Figure C. The capture of the remaining white stones is obvious on the next move. Even if the White tries to defend his three white stones by playing at 1 as shown in Figure D, on the next play Black at 2 can capture all the white stones.

Diagram 31, Figures A and B are further examples of this kind. Both white groups are dead. In Figure A, the three white stones are in check. Black can kill them by playing 1 as shown in Figure B. The Black groups shown in Figures C and D are also dead. One black stone is in check in each case, and if Black desires to defend it from capture he has to connect it to the main group. The group is thus reduced to a one-eyed group.

In actual games there are often groups of stones that at first glance seem to have two true eyes but are really open to attack. Frequently beginners find it hard to distinguish a real eye from a false eye.

The Black groups shown in Diagram 32 are dead although they have not yet been completely surrounded because they have only one real eye as they stand and there is no way for them to escape from the cordon of the opponent. In these cases, it is not necessary for White to fill up the vacant spaces in order to remove them from the board. They are regarded as dead before they are surrounded completely, and White can take them off the board at the end of the game without filling up those vacant intersections.

Life or death of a group of stones depends upon which player is to play first.

In the situation shown in Diagram 33, Figure A, if it

Diagram 31

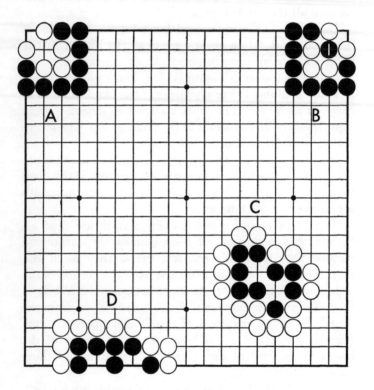

Diagram 32

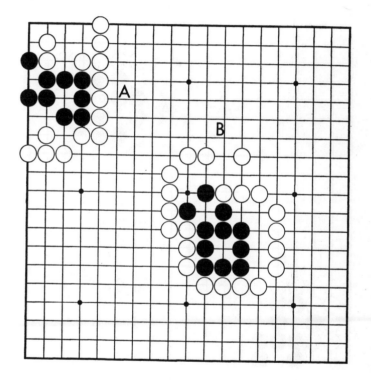

Diagram 33

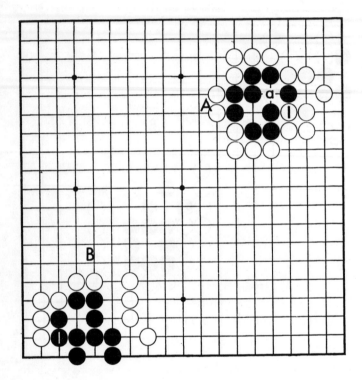

is White's turn to play and he plays 1, he can kill the black group of stones since the point "a" is false. If, on the other hand, it was Black's turn, he could save his group by playing at the same place.

Figure B merely shows another example of the same situation. Depending upon which side plays first, the whole black group of stones can or cannot be saved. If Black plays first, the life of the group is obviously saved by playing at 1 as indicated.

Look at Diagram 34 carefully. This is to show how you can kill a group of stones by rendering the group hopeless because of a false eye. Where do you have to play in order to kill the black group of stones in this diagram?

The play at 1 as shown in Figure B is correct, and you can, in so doing, kill the whole group because the point at 1 is a false eye. However, if, by mistake, you play at 1 as indicated in Figure C, you can never kill this group because it now has two separate eyes by Black playing at 2.

Diagram 35 is another example of a false eye. All of the black stones will be killed if White is to play first, although at first sight this may not be apparent. The proper sequence of play for White is as shown in Figure B ("a" is false). If, on the other hand, it is Black's turn, he can save his group by playing at 1 as indicated in Figure C.

There is another important rule you must learn about the life or death of a group of stones.

Groups of stones which contain vacant spaces can be lost or saved depending on whether or not two separate eyes can be formed in those spaces. Diagram 36, Figure A, is an example of this. The point marked "1" is a real eye, and you can definitely make another eye at the

Diagram 34

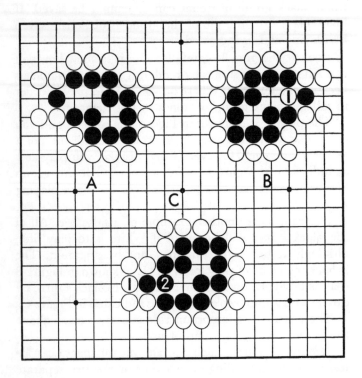

Diagram 35

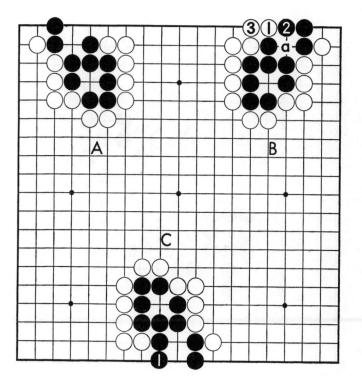

Diagram 36

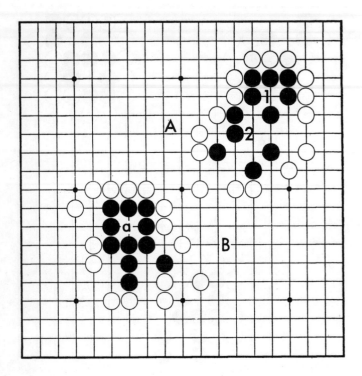

point marked "2." Figure B shows a hopeless group of stones which cannot form an additional eye. It contains one real eye as it stands but there is no possibility of forming another. This can be proved by studying the previous example shown in Diagram 33. The group can make nothing but a false eye.

The four black groups in Diagram 37 can form two separate eyes if Black plays first at the points marked "a." If, on the contrary, White plays first, he can kill these groups by playing at the same point.

To test your understanding thus far, try to solve the situation in Diagram 38, Figure A, before reading further.

White is safe even though Black plays first in this situation. If Black enters at "a," White saves by playing at "b"; if Black plays at "b," White plays at "a" and thus has two eyes. Figures B and C show you the same situations as this. In both situations shown therein, if Black plays at "a," White plays at "b"; if Black plays at "b," White plays at "a" and thus makes two separate eyes. You now understand clearly that these white groups cannot be killed even if Black plays first. However, the situation shown in Figure D is quite different from the previous situations. If it is Black's turn to play, he can kill the white group by playing at 1. If White plays at 2, Black plays at 3, thus rendering White hopeless to make two eyes. If White can play first, White can play to 1, thus making two eyes.

A few more examples are shown in Diagram 39. In Figure A, if Black plays at 1, he can kill the white group, while White to the same point would form four eyes. Figure B is a position somewhat similar to the last. If

Diagram 37

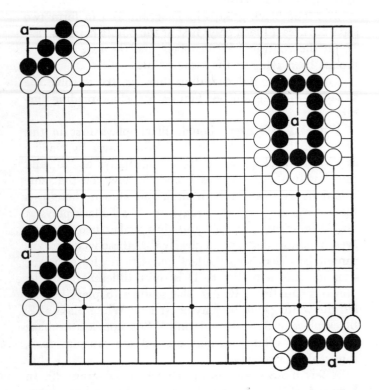

Diagram 38

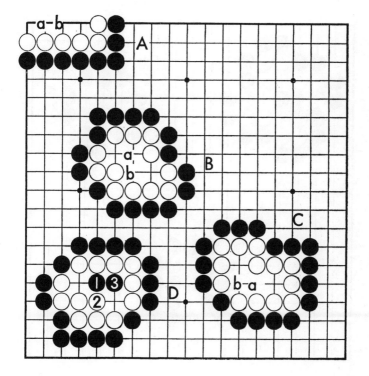

Diagram 39

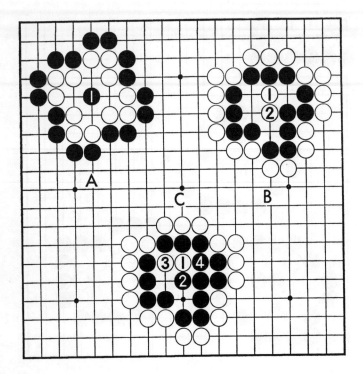

White plays at 1 and is permitted to follow with 2, then Black cannot be saved. Therefore, upon White's playing at 1, Black must at once play at 2, thereby being able to defend his group. If White continues to play at 3 as indicated in Figure C, Black simply joins at 4 and is safe.

There exist many more types of "safe and dead" groups of stones other than those shown and explained in this chapter. However, it is very hard to master all of them in a short period of time. It is suggested that you make progress by study or by seeking the assistance of an advanced player. The knowledge acquired through close study of the examples shown in this chapter will illustrate the principle and will prove of immeasurable value.

Diagram 40

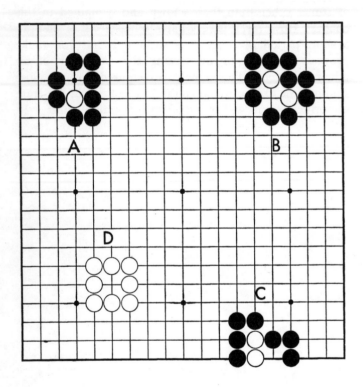

· 7 ·

Illegal Plays

In Chapter 2, you learned that you may play on any vacant point of intersection of the board which you desire to occupy except as stated in Rule 6. However, there are some illegal plays which are exceptions.

Rule 6 provides that neither player is permitted to place a stone on a point that is completely surrounded by the opponent if there is only the one point vacant, unless that play results in the capture of some of the surrounding stones. In other words, it is forbidden to place any stone in a position which deprives it of liberty.

In Diagram 40, Figures A, B, and C, White is forbidden to play at the one remaining vacancy because all of these plays leave the white stones involved without liberty. For the very same reason, Black is forbidden to play on the center of the white group D.

However, Diagram 41 illustrates that White can play on a point that was forbidden in the preceding diagram because if he does this he can capture part or all of the black stones and also obtain a liberty for his stone. The results of such play are seen in Diagram 42.

Diagram 41

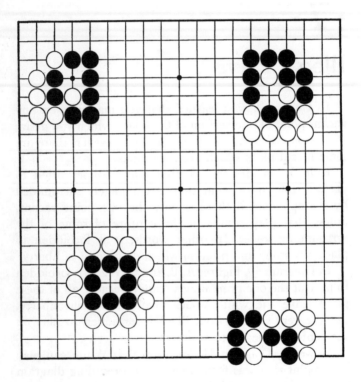

Diagram 42

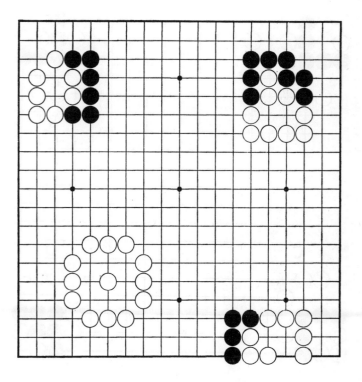

Diagram 43

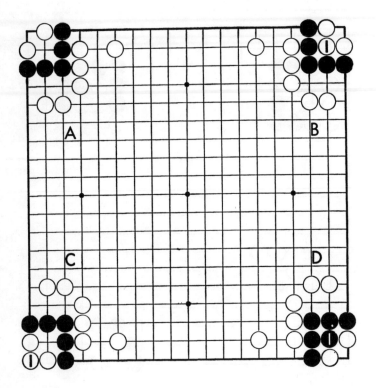

In Diagram 43, Figure A, if it is White's turn to play, he can prevent Black from making two eyes by playing as indicated in Figures B or C. If, on the other hand, it is Black's play, he can save his group by playing at 1 as in Figure D, for it is now impossible for White to play on the corner. Of course, Black can play on the corner since he then captures two white stones.

Diagram 44

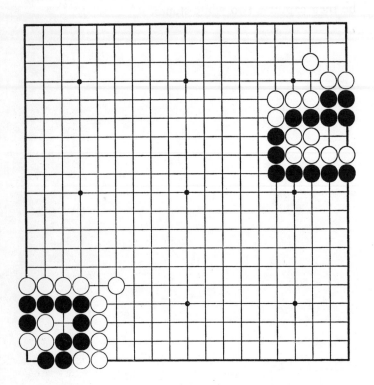

·8·

SEKI Situation

It is now time to study the situation called *seki* which may be translated as "a neutral position."

It sometimes happens that a series of plays will develop into an impasse or draw, and, when this occurs, the area involved is neutralized, ignored, and omitted from scoring calculations.

Such positions as are shown in Diagram 44 demonstrate *seki* situations. It may be seen that neither side can enter without at once losing stones on the next move of the opponent. However, the outer walls being open to attack, there always exists the chance of their being captured. In that case, the *seki* situation is broken up and capture effected in the usual way.

Diagram 45, Figure A, shows another *seki* situation. If Black in this situation plays at either one of the two vacant points, White captures four black stones as shown in Figures B and C, subsequently making the necessary two eyes by playing either at "a" or "b." If Black plays at "a," White must play at "b," otherwise Black will do so and eventually capture all of the white stones. In order

Diagram 45

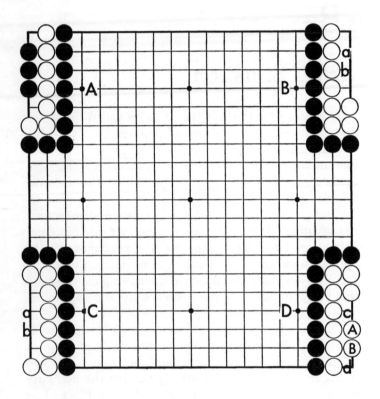

Diagram 46

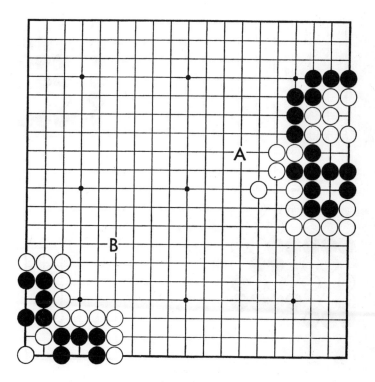

Diagram 47

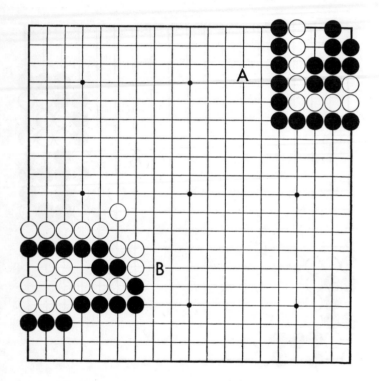

to capture them, the following steps are used. Black plays either at "c" or "d" as shown in Figure D, and then White captures three black stones because the white group is in check. Black plays again, placing a stone upon the middle point of three left vacant so as to prevent two separate eyes in the white group.

Here are some other examples of *seki* position. In both situations shown in Diagram 46, Figures A and B, neither can attack the other without risking certain death. All vacant points inside the surrounding walls are regarded as neutral territories which cannot be counted or claimed by the players. There are, of course, many *more* seki situations but by now you should generally understand what they are and recognize those which may occur in actual games.

However, the situation shown in Diagram 47, Figure A is quite different from those previously shown although this may not be apparent to you. It is clearly seen that the black group has an eye on the corner but the white group doesn't. The position is now no longer *seki,* but is called by the Japanese *me ari me nashi,* or literally "having an eye, not having an eye." In this case, the white stones are dead because if Black plays at either one of two adjacent vacant points, White cannot kill the black stones by playing at the remaining vacancy, for the reason that the vacant eye is still left vacant. Figure B merely shows another example of this.

Diagram 48

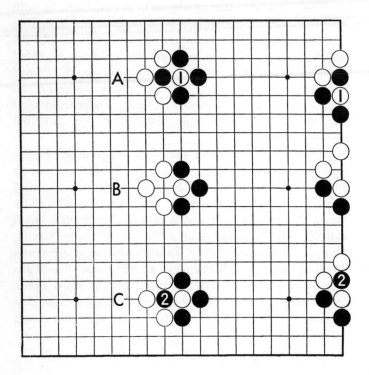

·9·

KO Situation

There is one exception to the rule that players may place their stones on any vacant points of intersection. This rule is called *ko* and is one of the most interesting features of the game. An example is shown in Diagram 48.

Assuming that it is White's turn to play, he can play 1 as shown in Figure A and can take the one black stone which is already surrounded on three sides, and the position shown in Figure B would then result. It is now obvious that the white stone which has just been played is surrounded by three black stones. If, as in Figure C, Black captures this white stone, we are back to the position we started with in Figure A. If the players were permitted to take stones by repeating moves in this way, the game would be endless. In order to allow the game to continue, the following rule was established when a player has captured an enemy stone in a *ko* position, his opponent may not recapture until he first makes at least one play elsewhere on the board.

This rule not only prevents the above situation but

Diagram 49

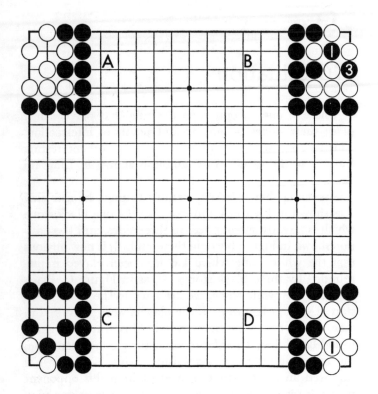

it also adds interest to the play. When a player is thus prevented from retaking a stone, he tries to play in another area where he can attack a larger group of stones than is involved in the situation where *ko* occurs. In this way he forces his opponent to follow him, after which he can return to retake the stone in *ko*.

The three examples on the right in Diagram 48 show the same situation as previously mentioned. In this elementary *ko* situation, there is but one stone involved. However, in actual games the outcome of a *ko* fight concerns the life or death of large groups of stones and often decides the results of the game.

In the situation shown in Diagram 49, Figure A, if it is Black's turn to play, he will undoubtedly play 1 as shown in Figure B and thereby capture the white stone in *ko*. Four white stones are in check. Although it is now White's turn, he is not permitted to retake the black stone immediately but he must first play somewhere else on the board. If Black on his next move, regardless of where White may have played, captures the four white stones in check by playing at 3, the resulting position will be as indicated in Figure C. He has thus acquired territory valued at a total of 15 points as indicated in the following computation: (Eight points indicate captured intersections.)

8 points + 5 captured stones + 2 dead stones = 15 points

As you learned in the previous chapter, these captured stones are used to fill up the vacant spaces claimed by the opponent, and, therefore, each of those stones is counted as 1 point. It is needless to say that the two dead stones which are left in the corner can be removed from the board at the end of the game.

Diagram 50

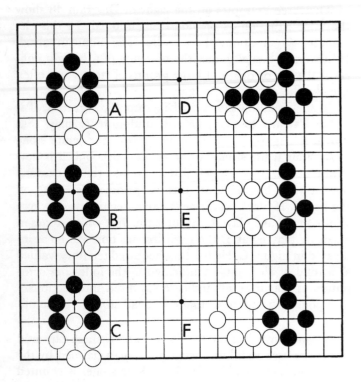

On the contrary, however, if White can play first in the situation shown in Figure A, he can doubtless fill in *ko* with the play as shown in Figure D and thereby form two separate eyes, making his group of stones permanently safe from attack.

A situation which sometimes is mistaken for *ko* occurs when a player takes more than one stone and the stone thus played is threatened on three sides. In this case, the opponent retakes at once because it is obvious that an endless series of moves will not ensue.

Diagram 50 illustrates this. In the example shown in Figure A, Black can take two white stones with the results indicated in Figure B. In this case, White can immediately retake the one black stone as in Figure C for the reason above mentioned. A similar situation is shown in Figures D, E, and F for your study. It should not be difficult for you to understand these examples.

Diagram 51

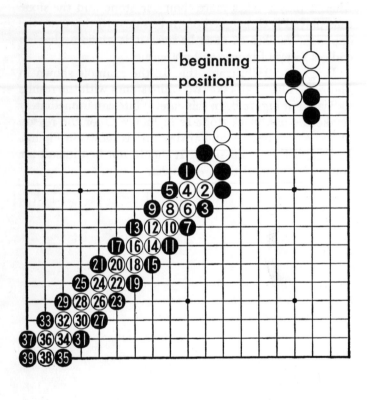

·10·

Basic Tactics

Inasmuch as *go* is a game of strategy, in which there are many tactical procedures, it is necessary for beginners to learn at least some of the fundamental basic tactics. You should be able to master them without much difficulty if you remember what you have learned in the previous chapters.

Set forth below are some of the tactics needed to meet situations that develop during play.

In Diagram 51 it is Black's play and he must play at 1, whereupon White attempts to live by playing at 2. Black has to play at 3, and the subsequent steps are taken as recorded. This results in the capture of the white stones upon reaching the edge of the board. This situation is called *shicho* which means "a running attack."

Therefore when such a position develops a shrewd player would not extend his losses in this way but would instead play elsewhere, abandoning temporarily the threatened stone.

On the other hand, however, the case is not hopeless if there is a friendly stone in the line of flight, no matter

Diagram 52

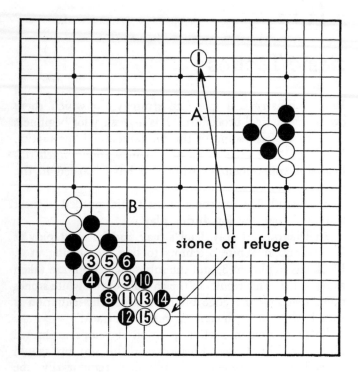

stone of refuge

Diagram 53

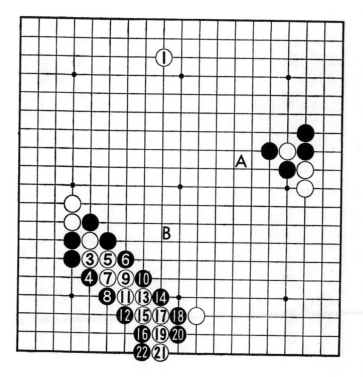

Diagram 54

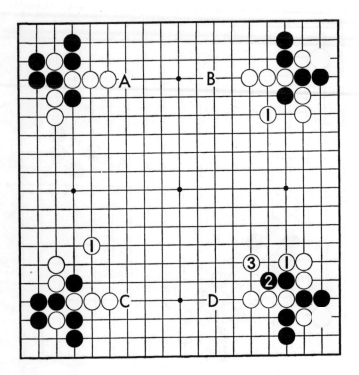

how far off it may be. This stone is called *shicho atari,* which may be translated as "a stone of refuge from a running attack." A study of Diagram 52 shows the truth of this. As you can see, Black cannot capture the white stones in a *shicho,* because the threatened white stones are eventually connected with the stone of refuge as shown in Figure B. The single white stone marked as 1 in Figure A is the stone of refuge.

If Black fails to notice the meaning of this white stone and plays at some other place on the board, White immediately attempts to escape by playing at 3 and eventually succeeds in connecting to the white single stone above mentioned. In this situation Black should not have tried to capture the white stone in this manner because now his own stones are in a position to be attacked by White in many directions.

In the situation shown in Diagram 53, Figure A, the waiting white stone is not posted on the line of progress, in which case the running attack is successful as indicated in Figure B. White must be careful not to misplace the stone of refuge in an attempt to escape from the running attack.

There are many ways for White to prevent the black stone from escape in Diagram 54, Figure A. The plays in Figures B and C are correct and these plays are called *geta,* which may be translated as "capping" plays. Figure D is a *shicho* which you have already learned: if Black tries to escape by playing at 2, White, needless to say, plays at 3, a capping play.

Diagram 55 is another example of a capping play. In this situation, there is no possibility for Black to find a way to escape. Figures B and C show you the truth of this.

Diagram 55

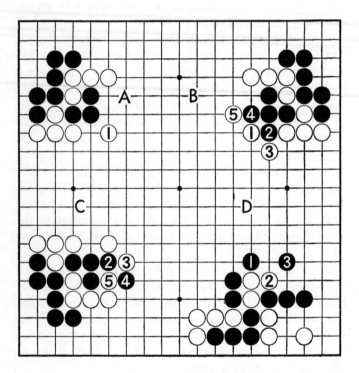

Diagram 56

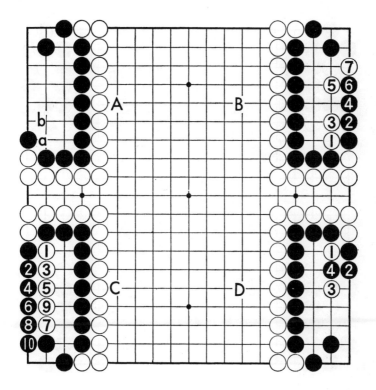

Diagram 57

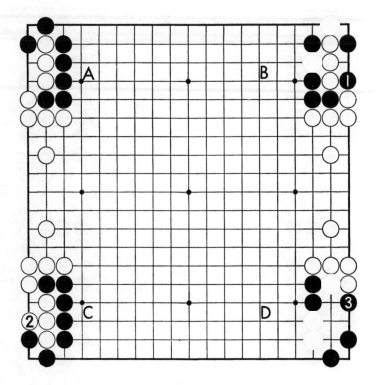

Similar cases frequently occur in actual games. If you memorize these plays, you will find no difficulty in preventing the escape of your opponent's stones.

Another example of a capping play is shown in Figure D, and from this example you should learn why the Black at 1 and 3 are essential in order to prevent the flight of the hostile stone.

In the situation shown in Diagram 56, Figure A, Black must make an additional play either at "a" or "b" in order to defend his territory completely. If Black fails to do so, the one black stone will be captured by a capping play as shown in Figure B, resulting in a big loss of Black's territory. Figures C and D show two incorrect plays for White, in which cases Black loses nothing and, on the contrary, the white stones are dead.

In the situation shown in Diagram 57, Figure A, if it is Black's turn to play, he must play 1 as in Figure B, thus threatening the three white stones. White may reply by playing at 2 and captures the one black stone previously placed as indicated in Figure C, but Black will again play at 3 (the same point as played in Figure B) and he captures the four white stones as in Figure D since they have been completely enclosed by White's last move. Black's play is called *uttegae* which means "sacrifice play." It is incorrect for Black to play at 1 as in Diagram 58, Figure A, for then White promptly joins by playing at 2 as in Figure B, threatening the two black stones. If Black attempts to save them by playing at 3 as in Figure C, White can capture the four black stones by playing at "a." If, on the other hand, it is White's turn to play in the initial situation, he must play 1 as shown in Figure D, thus preventing capture as indicated in Diagram 57.

Diagram 58

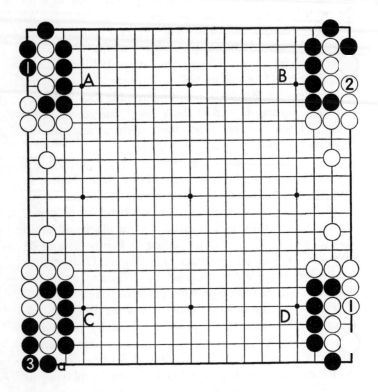

Diagram 59

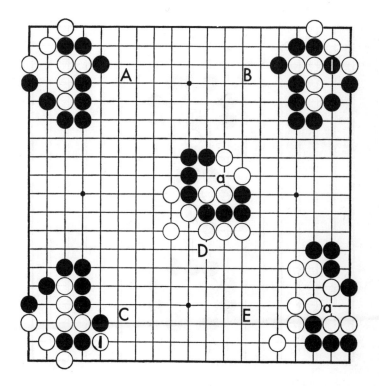

Diagram 60

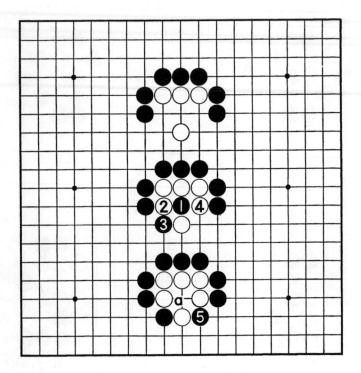

Diagram 59 shows another example of sacrifice play. If it is Black's turn to play in this situation, he plays 1 as indicated in Figure B and the four white stones are in check. If White plays as shown in Diagram 57 and captures the one sacrifice black stone, Black re-enters and captures the five which are enclosed. The remaining three need not be removed though they are dead; they can be taken off the board at the end of the game. On the contrary, if White can play first, he plays 1 as in Figure C, capturing the two black stones. He can now make the necessary eyes with little difficulty.

Two more examples of these situations are shown in Figures D and E. If it is Black's turn to play in these situations, he plays at the point marked "a" and thereby captures the two white stones. On the contrary, if White can play first, he can save his two stones by playing at the same point.

In the situation shown in Diagram 60, all three white stones will be killed if it is Black's turn to play. Black plays 1. White tries to escape by playing at 2. Black then plays at 3, and now the four white stones are in check. White attempts to avoid capture by playing at 4, capturing one black stone. Black continues by playing at 5, again threatening. If White fills the point at "a," Black can capture all the seven white stones. This position is called *tsuru no sugomori,* which literally means "the confinement of cranes to their nest."

If it is White's turn to play in Diagram 61, Figure A, how can he save his five stones? The correct method is shown in Figures B and C. White must check two black stones first by playing at 1 and Black then connects with 2. The next move of White is important. He must pitch

Diagram 61

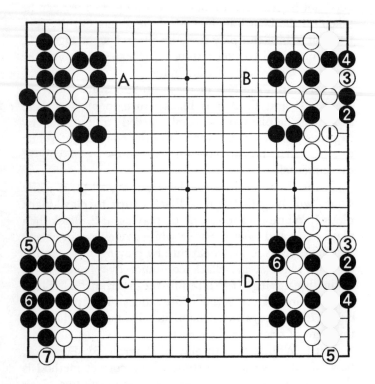

Diagram 62

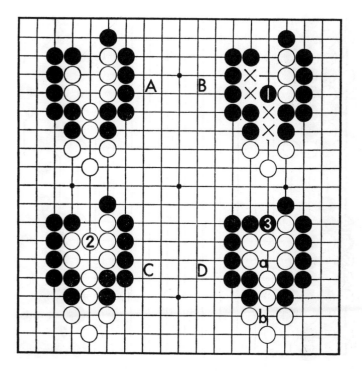

Diagram 63

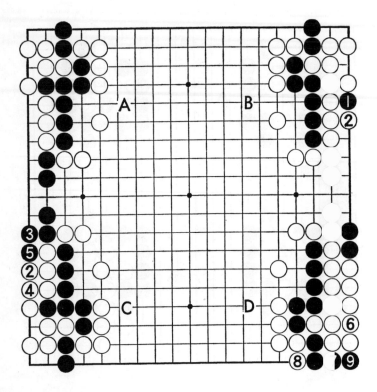

in a stone at 3 and let Black capture it with 4. White then checks four black stones by playing at 5, and if Black attempts to avoid capture by connecting at 6, White gives a check at 7. It is now easily seen that there is no way for Black to escape capture. However, if White neglects to sacrifice a stone as he did in Figure B, he accomplishes nothing but loses his own five stones as in Figure D.

Diagrams 62 and 63 show two more examples of sacrifice plays. In the situation shown in Diagram 62, Figure A, if it is Black's turn to play, he must sacrifice a stone by playing at 1 as shown in Figure B, and now the four white stones marked "X" are in check. White attempts to avoid capture by playing at 2 as in Figure C, capturing the one black stone. Black then threatens the six white stones by playing at 3 as in Figure D. If White fills the point at "a," Black can capture the nine white stones on his next move at "b." If however, White can play first in the original situation, he can save them by playing at the same point as Black did in Figure B because he can now connect at the point marked "b" whenever threatened.

In the situation shown in Diagram 63, Figure A, if it is Black's turn to play, he can save his seven stones, which seem to be unable to escape from the cordon of the white group, by playing as follows. First Black must play 1, threatening the one white stone. White replies with 2 and captures the one black stone. Black then plays 3. If White, on his next move, replies by playing at 4 in order to save his four stones, Black then plays at 5 and thereby threatens the six white stones. If White connects them with his comrade by playing at 6, Black can capture the eleven white stones by playing at 7 and 9 as shown in Figure D.

Diagram 64

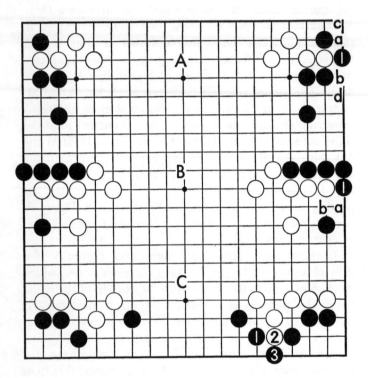

Diagram 64 shows some joining methods on the edge of the board. In each illustration, if Black plays 1, he can join his two groups of stones. Black's play at 1 is called *watari*, which literally means "crossing over." Let's examine each situation in detail and ascertain why White cannot break Black's joining after playing at 1. In the situation shown in Figure A, if White plays either "a" or "b," he will be immediately killed by Black at "c" or "d." In Figure B, if White attempts to advance by playing at "a," Black replies with "b," if White plays "b," Black then replies with "a." In Figure C, if White tries to advance by playing at 2, Black can avoid it by playing at 3. White henceforth cannot break Black's connection because of the reason shown in Figure A.

Diagram 65

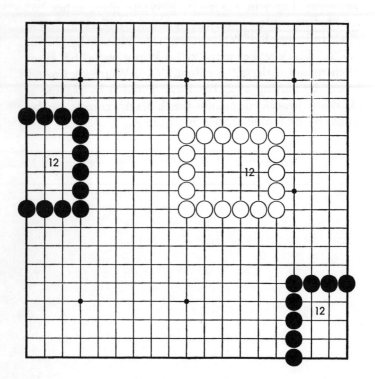

· 11 ·

Playing the Game

As you have completed a study of the rules, tactics, and objectives of *go,* you are now ready to learn some of the game's mechanics.

The game is commenced by playing in or around the corners of the board. The reason for this, as has been pointed out, is that the corners are the easiest areas in which to form territory and the simplest to defend. The next most advantageous sections are the sides, while the center of the board is the most difficult area in which to form territory. This fact is sufficiently proved by the figures shown in Diagram 65. Each of the groups has surrounded twelve points of territory. However, you will quickly observe that these territories have not been formed with the same number of stones:

Corner	———————	8 stones
Side	———————	12 stones
Center	———————	18 stones

Obviously, it is easier to form territory in the corners of the board than any other place. Such being the case,

Diagram 66

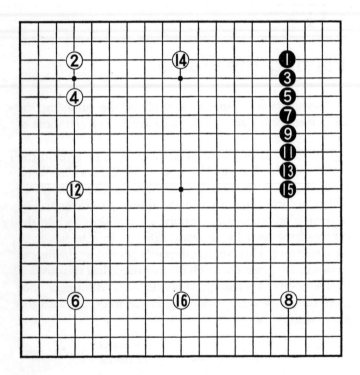

in an ordinary game the play generally proceeds from the corners and edges to the center. However, other factors than the acquisition of territory must be considered. Maneuverability towards the center is one of them. Nevertheless, the principle illustrated in Diagram 65 is a basic fundamental of the game.

Study Diagram 66 and you will note that Black with his first plays up to 15 has sequestered about 30 points of territory. But while he was devoting himself to one specific territory, White has ranged widely over the rest of the board with a potential area worth many times the amount of territory acquired by Black. This indicates that you must pay attention to the entire board, and it is wise to outline loosely your desired territories in the beginning.

Diagram 67 shows an example of correct opening procedure, although there are many other ways actually used at this stage of the game. The players moved first toward the corners where they either protected their corner or prevented the opponent from fortifying a corner.

There are several fundamental ways to play in or around the corners and Diagram 68 shows some of these. A stone placed on the intersection of the third and fourth lines from the edge of the board is called *komoku* in Japanese and it is the most flexible of all corner placements. Generally, three major methods are used for corner placements with *komoku*. Black's play at 1 shown in Figure A is called *keima* or *kogeima* which is similar to the knight's move in chess. This placement is called *kogeima shimari*. If the stones are one point farther apart as shown in Figure B, it is called *ogeima* which means "the great knight's move." The placement illustrated in Figure C is called *ikken shimari*. *Ikken* means "skipping one point."

Diagram 67

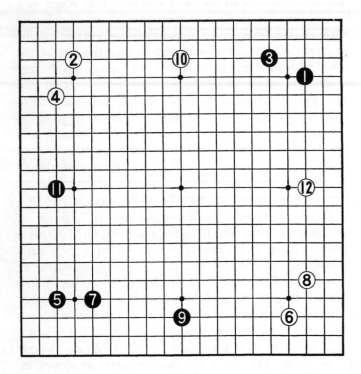

Figure D shows a corner placement from the stone on the intersection of the fourth line from both edges of the board. You can also play at "a" or "b" as in the foregoing figures.

The opening play of the game is very important, however, and in order to acquire adequate knowledge of this, actual playing experience is necessary. It is not the purpose of this introductory booklet to teach the more complicated strategy. A careful study of the foregoing "Steppingstones" will enable the interested reader to enjoy the ancient game of *go* and lead him to further study.

Diagram 68

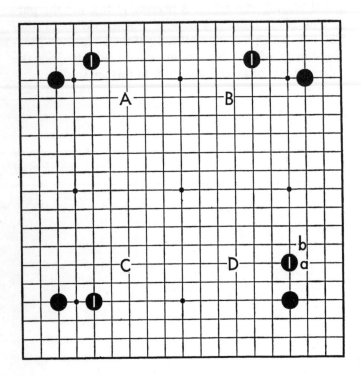

Problems

White to play.   How can Black group be killed?

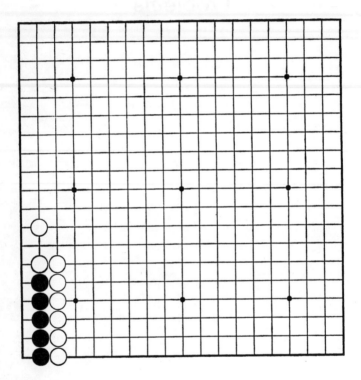

Problem 2

White to play. How can Black group be killed?

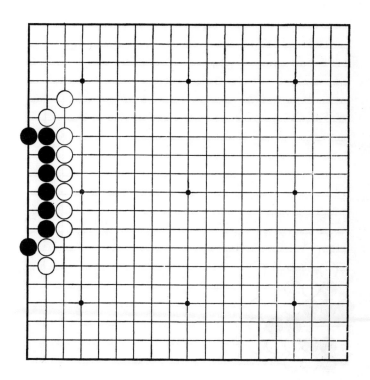

White to play.   How can Black group be killed?

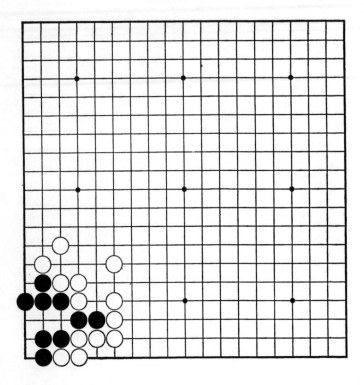

Problem 4

White to play.   How can Black group be killed?

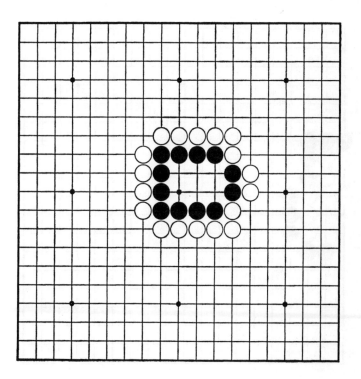

Problem 5

Black to play.   How can White group be killed?

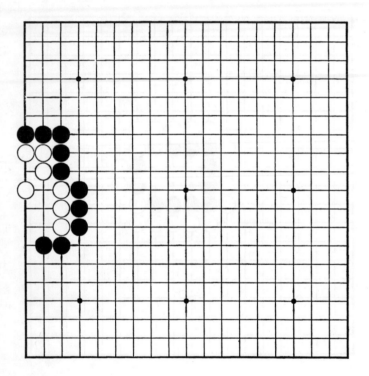

Problem 6

White to play. How can Black group be killed?

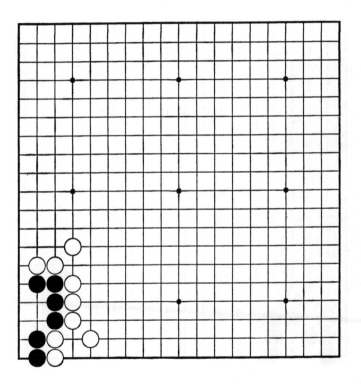

Problem 7

White to play. How can Black group be killed?

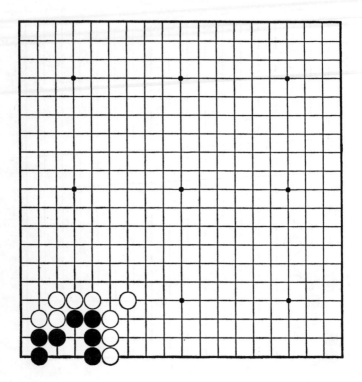

Problem 8

White to play. How can Black group be killed?

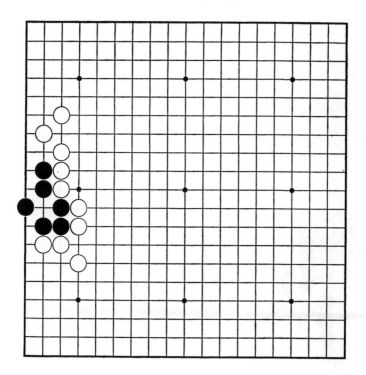

Problem 9

Black to play. The four black stones have only one escape from this trap. What is it?

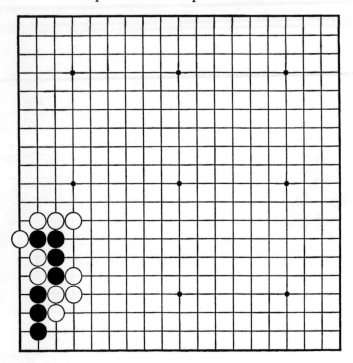

Problem 10

Black to play.   Three disconnected Black groups can be
connected by capturing some White stones.   How?

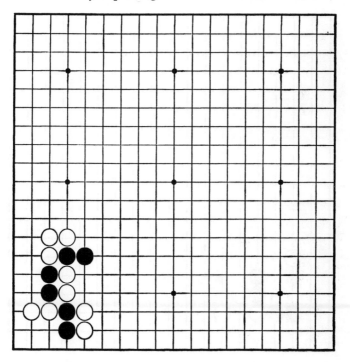

Problem 11

Black to play. How can White stone "A" be captured?
(It cannot be taken by *shicho*.)

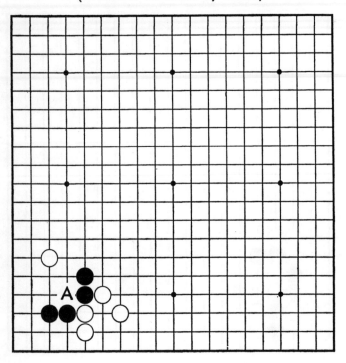

Problem 12

White to play.   Two Black stones can be captured. How?

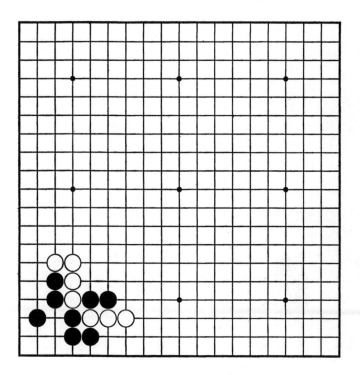

Problem 13

Black to play. How can the single
White stone be captured?

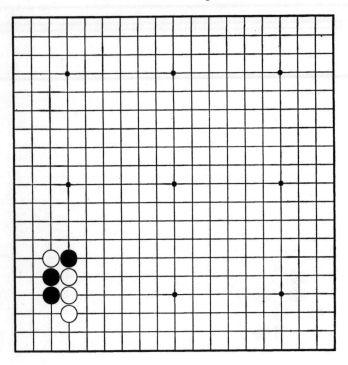

Problem 14

Black to play. How can the three Black stones in the corner be connected with the other group?

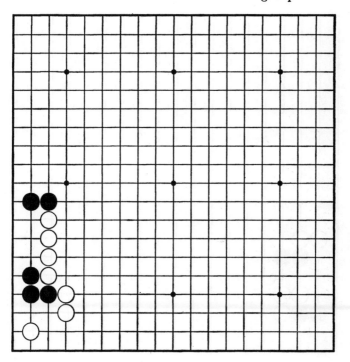

Problem 15

Black to play.   How can the two Black groups
be connected?

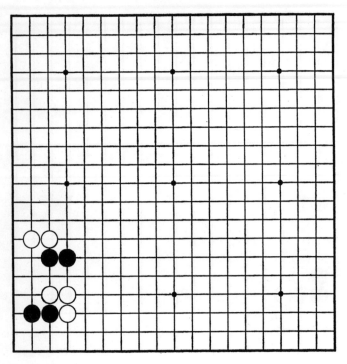

White to play.   Black's corner territory is still incomplete.
How can it be broken up?

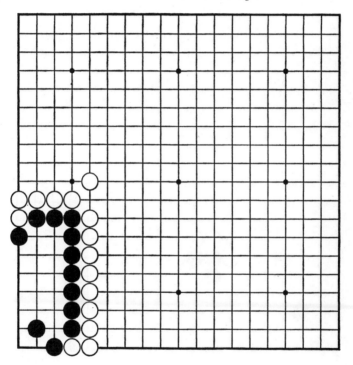

Problem 17

White to play. Using *shicho*, can the Black stones be captured?

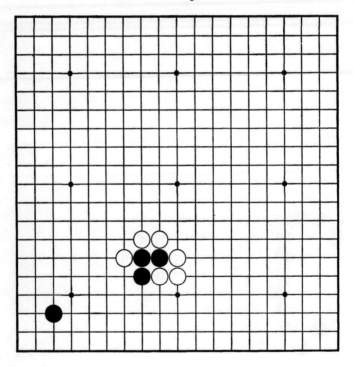

Black to play.   The four White stones on the corner
can be captured.   How ?

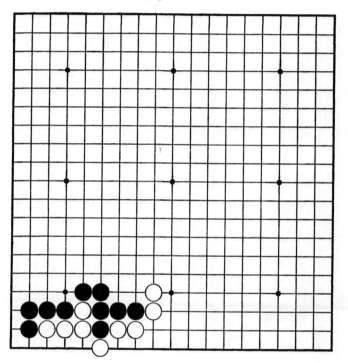

Problem 19

White to play. Three White stones are in danger. Using sacrifice play, they can be saved by capturing the Black stone on the corner. How?

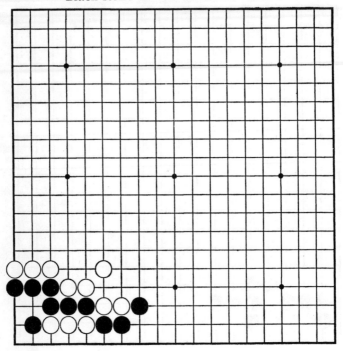

Problem 20

Black to play. How can the Black group be saved?

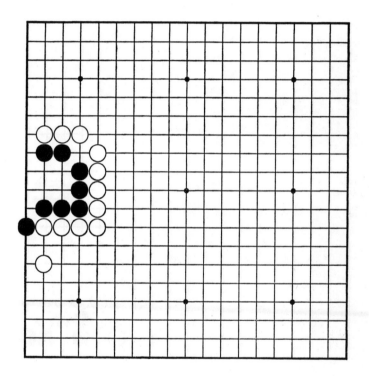

Problem 21

White to play.   How can the Black group be killed?

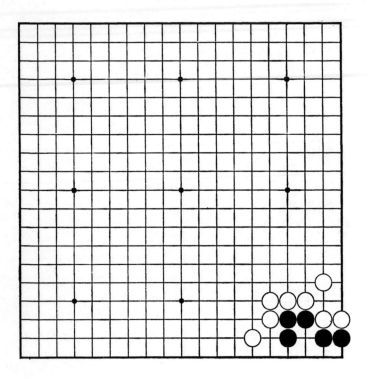

Problem 22

White to play.　How can the Black group be killed?

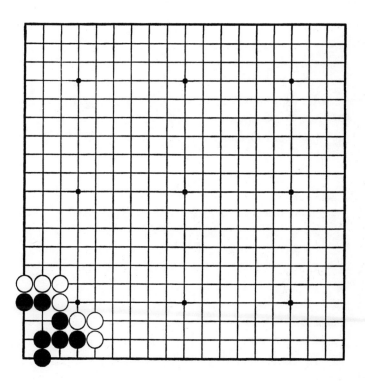

Solutions

Solution 1 (a)

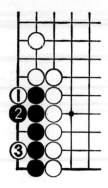

Solution 1 (b)

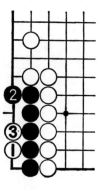

Solution 2 (a)

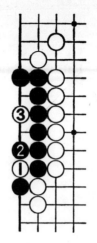

Solution 2 (b)

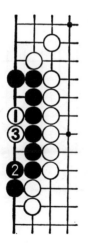

Solution 3 (a)

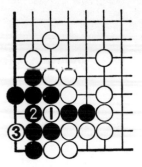

Solution 3 (b)

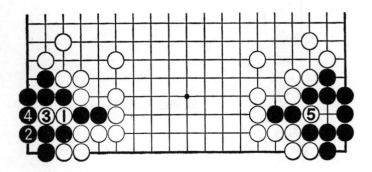

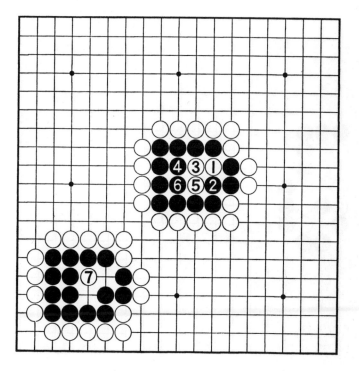

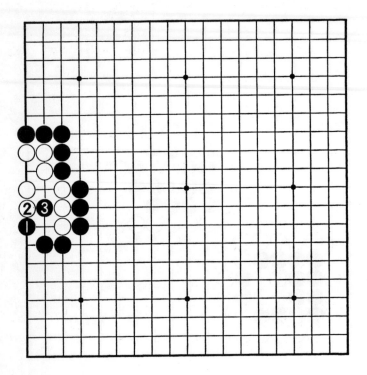

Solution 6 (a)

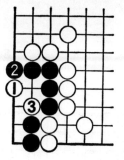

Solution 6 (b)

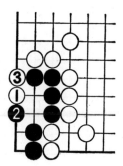

Solution 7

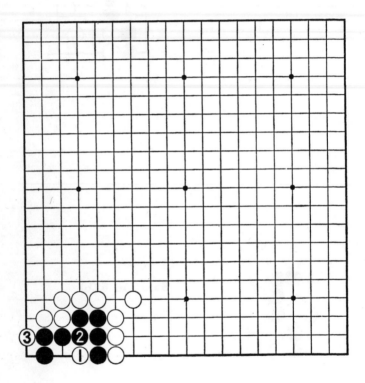

Solution 8

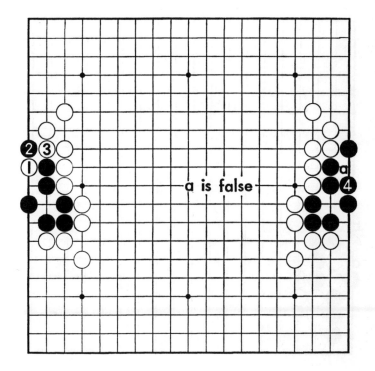

Solution 9

If White plays "a", all four stones can be
captured when Black plays "b"

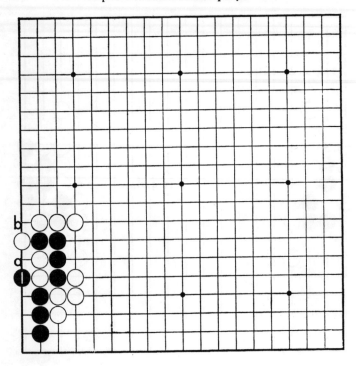

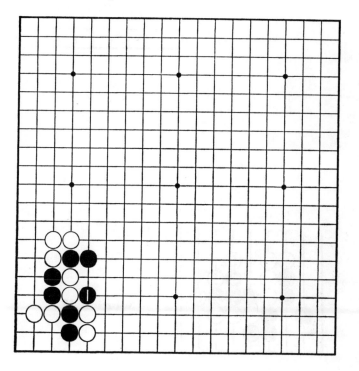

Solution 11

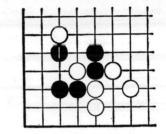

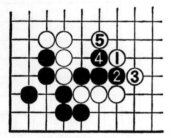

Solution 12

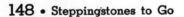

Solution 13

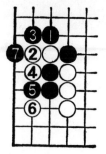

Solution 14

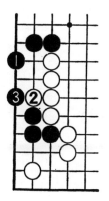

Solution 15

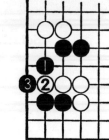

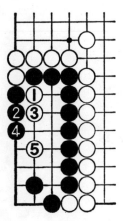

Solution 16

Solution 17

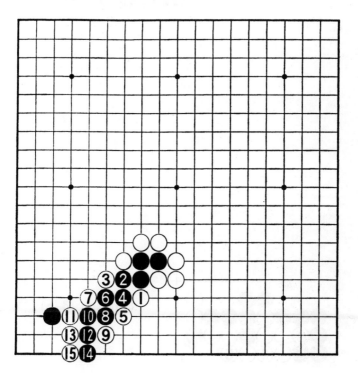

Solution 18 (a)

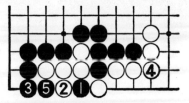

Solution 18 (b)

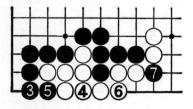

Solution 19

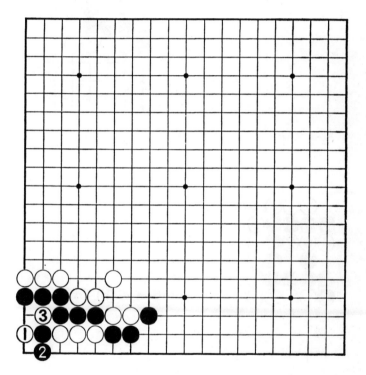

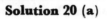

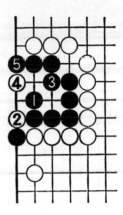

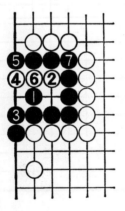

Solution 20 (b) *Seki*

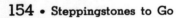

Solution 21 (a)

White's play at 1 is the
place to kill Black

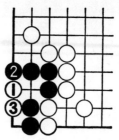

Solution 21 (b)

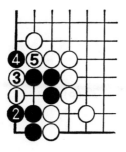

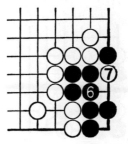

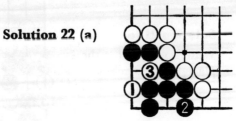

Solution 22 (a)

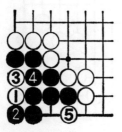

Solution 22 (b)

The End of the Game

Diagram 69

The end of a game between a
professional and a leading amateur

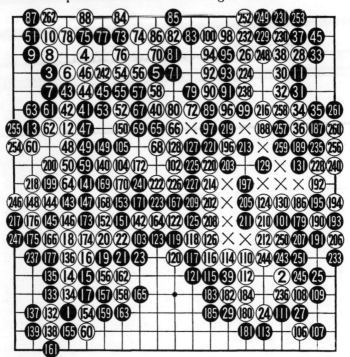

198 (white) 201 (black) and 204 (white) take *ko*

178 (white) was placed where 145 (black) is now

234 (white) was placed where 193 (black) is now, to terminate *ko* situation

239 (black) was placed where 96 (white) is now, to terminate *ko* situation

X=neutral territory filled in

Diagram 70

A board arranged for counting purposes.

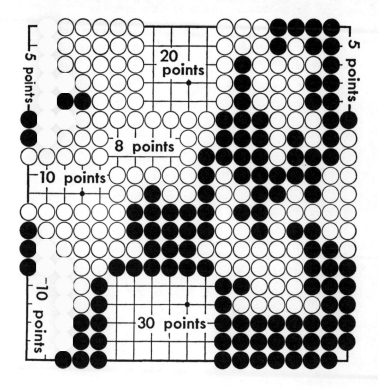